PupStyle

Red Carpet Pups

By Dara Foster

SCHOLASTIC INC.

I dedicate this book to my daughters, Parker and Ripley.
Thank you for your endless giggles and creative ideas.

Special thanks to Melissa Gampel at DoggieCoutureShop.com
for supplying pet fashion and accessories for this book and Carlene Mahanna
for her pet fashion styling assistance and endless devotion to PupStyle.

Dog model casting, pet fashion styling, and art direction by Dara Foster.
Photography by Mats Rudels.

Credits:
Front cover: dog model Toshi San, sunglasses by Doggles, white dress shirt by Gidget Gear, black biker jacket by VIPoochy; back cover: Cee-Lo Green dog model Sylvia, black T-shirt by Dog In The Closet, Taylor Swift dog model Princess Grace, Marilyn Monroe dress by Pink Hot Dog, gold sandals by Love Long Long; p. 7: dog model Bella Grace, Spike wig by Wiggles, sunglasses by Doggles, denim stars jacket by Puppy Love, black tee by Zack & Zoey, green camo sneakers by Bella Bark & Meow; p. 11: dog model Bella, custom-made dress by pet fashion designer Kelly Owens Couture, custom-made blue wig by Wiggles; p. 15: dog model Monster, blue satin dress by Nina's Couture Closet, leopard boots by Doggy Style Designs; p. 19: dog model Princess Giana, custom-made dress by pet fashion designer Linda Higgins, sneakers by Love Long Long; p. 23: dog model Jackson, necktie by Doggie Design, Egyptian cotton dress shirt by Gidget Gear; p. 27: dog model Princess Grace, Marilyn Monroe dress by Pink Hot Dog, gold sandals by Love Long Long; p. 31: dog model Ganji, custom-made gray suit jacket and orange shirt by Tiny Paws Couture, fedora hat by Sew Doggy Style; p. 35: dog model Paddy, custom-made dress by pet fashion designer Linda Higgins, pink curly wig by Wiggles; p. 39: dog models Kiki Liu and Emmet, custom black Angelina dress by pet fashion designer Linda Higgins, custom wig by Wiggles, Brad Pitt tux by Carlene Mahanna, custom Brad Pitt wig by Wiggles; p. 43: dog model Zara, custom-made dress by pet fashion designer Linda Higgins, wig by Dara Foster; p. 47: dog model Sylvia, black T-shirt by Dog in the Closet; p. 50: dog model Toshi San, sunglasses by Doggles, white dress shirt by Gidget Gear, black biker jacket by VIPoochy; p. 55: dog model Madison, custom-made dress by pet fashion designer Linda Higgins, black beaded necklace from PupStyle by Dara Foster; p. 59: dog model Vivi, custom-made dress by pet fashion designer Linda Higgins; p. 63: photographer Jesse Freidin, dog model Gunther the American Pit Bull Terrier.
Backgrounds/other photos: front cover, top right (Nicki Minaj): © Patrick McMullan.com via AP Images; back cover, top right (Cee-Lo Green): © Gregg DeGuire/Picture Group via AP Images; back cover, top right (cash for gold): © iStockphoto; back cover, center (Taylor Swift): © Gregg DeGuire/Getty Images; back cover, bottom (guitar): © iStockphoto; p. 3 (Bo Obama): © Charles Dharapak/AP Photo; p. 5 (Justin Bieber): © Chris Pizzello/AP Photo; p. 7 (microphone): © iStockphoto; p. 9 (Katy Perry): © Kevin Mazur/WireImage/Getty Images; p. 11 (lollipops): © iStockphoto; p. 13 (Victoria Justice): © Gregg DeGuire/Picture Group via AP Images; p. 15 (red carpet): © iStockphoto; p. 17 (Kristen Stewart): © Jeffrey Mayer/Wire Image/Getty Images; p. 19 (meadow): © iStockphoto; p. 21 (Taylor Lautner): © Anita Bugge/Wirelmage/Getty Images; p. 23 (red carpet): © iStockphoto; p. 25 (Taylor Swift): © Gregg DeGuire/FilmMagic/Getty Images; p. 27 (guitar): © iStockphoto; p. 29 (Bruno Mars): © Lester Cohen/WireImage/Getty Images; p. 31 (stage): © iStockphoto; p. 33 (Nicki Minaj): © PatrickMcMullan.com via AP Images; p. 35 (stage): © iStockphoto; p. 37 (Pitt/Jolie): © Jewel Samad/AFP/Getty Images; p. 39 (red carpet): © iStockphoto; p. 41 (Selena Gomez): © Gregg DeGuire/Picture Group via AP Images; p. 43 (stage): © iStockphoto; p. 45 (Cee-Lo): © Gregg DeGuire/PictureGroup via AP Images; p. 47 (gold): © iStockphoto; p. 49 (Zac Efron): © Joe Klamar/AFP/Getty Images; p. 51 (lighting): © iStockphoto; p. 53 (Keke Palmer): © Gregg DeGuire/Picture Group via AP Images; p. 55 (Christmas stars): © iStockphoto; p. 57 (Jennifer Lopez): © Matt Sayles/AP Photo; p. 59 (diamonds): © iStockphoto; p. 61 (Lady Gaga): © Joel Ryan/AP Photo; p. 63 (spotlights): © iStockphoto.

ISBN 978-0-545-53245-7

12 11 10 9 8 7 6 5 4 3 2   13 14 15 16 17

Printed in Malaysia 106
First printing, January 2013

Book Design by Marissa Asuncion

Some dogs, like the presidential pooch Bo, have celebrity status. Although not all dogs are famous, with a little bit of glam, any dog can be ready to rock the red carpet.

JUSTIN BIEBER

Justin Bieber is one lucky dog. When he's not selling out arenas, recording the hottest new song, or trying to stay in touch with millions of adoring fans (aka Beliebers), he gets to attend the coolest Hollywood events and travel all around the world.

MORKIE

Justin Bieber may have had one of the most famous haircuts ever, but dogs can have a signature style, too. The poodle has a very distinct cut with short hair on the body and long curly hair on the legs, tail, and head.

KATY PERRY

Katy Perry is a total animal lover. She even owns a cat named Kitty Perry. Although she may prefer cats to dogs, she always has a special place in her heart for one dog—Snoop Dogg!

BOSTON TERRIER

Cats and dogs may not always get along, but they do have quite a lot in common. They both have four paws, a very good sense of smell, and they also love being petted!

Victoria Justice can sing, act, and dance, which makes her a triple threat. This starlet is on top of the world with her own show, *Victorious*, on Nickelodeon. But before she was a celebrity, Victoria Justice did television commercials for Gap, Ovaltine, and many other companies.

TAN FRENCH BULLDOG

Some dogs are trained to be actors in commercials, television shows, and movies. Some of their tricks include rolling over, jumping, and barking on command.

Kristen Stewart shot to superstardom with her portrayal of Bella Swan in the *Twilight Saga* movies. Together, she and *Twilight* costar Robert Pattinson adopted a dog named Bear.

17

TRICOLOR CAVALIER KING CHARLES SPANIEL

Fans will line up for hours waiting to get an autograph from a celebrity. That's because they can meet their favorite celeb and get a unique autograph! Just like a celebrity's signature, every dog's paw print is one of a kind.

TAYLOR LAUTNER

Taylor Lautner made it onto Hollywood's hot list with his dramatic performances in the *Twilight Saga* movies. In the movies, he connected with his inner dog, as he portrayed the werewolf Jacob Black.

CONCORDE
FILMVERLEIH
EIN UNTERNEHMEN DER TELE MÜNCHEN GRUPPE
die twilight saga
eclipse
Bis zum Abendrot
AB 15. JULI IM KINO

PUG

Dogs are close relatives of wolves. It may be hard to believe, but many types of wolves are endangered.

America's Sweetheart, Taylor Swift is an actress, a spokesperson, and a musician. But she's best known for her incredible lyrics and her beautiful voice.

TOY POODLE

Just like their owners, dogs have voices too. Dogs can make over ten different sounds that range from a loud bark to a quiet whimper.

Bruno Mars may be known for his sweet voice, but he has an even sweeter side — he loves dogs! Bruno's dog's name is Geronimo.

COCKER SPANIEL

This dog is staying warm in his sleek blazer. Though dogs' natural coats help them stay warm, many nonshedding dogs need a jacket to keep warm in winter.

Nicki Minaj is a famous hip-hop artist with head-turning style. Part of her signature look is her ever-changing hair. One day she will wear a pink wig, and the next, green!

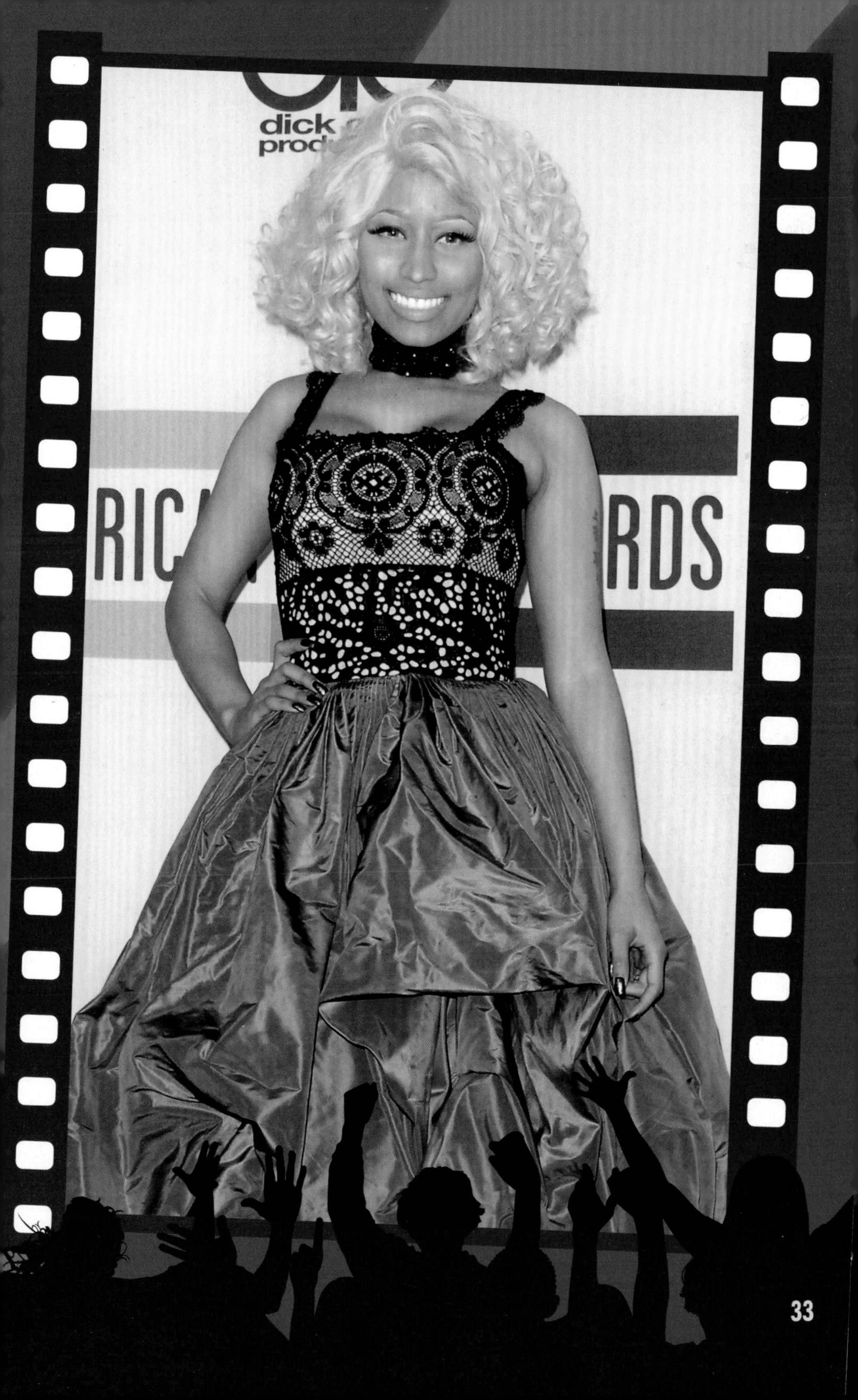

MORKIE

Dogs can come in many different colors from black to white to tan to gray. Some dogs, like the dalmatian, are known for their signature look. This Morkie, a mixture of a Maltese and a Yorkshire terrier, can be white like the Maltese, brown and gray like the Yorkshire terrier, or a mixture of both!

ANGELINA JOLIE AND BRAD PITT

Angelina and Brad are one of Hollywood's hottest couples. When they hit the red carpet at an awards show, all eyes are on them to see what they're wearing.

LONG-HAIRED CHIHUAHUAS

Move over, humans—dogs are strutting on the red carpet, too. With so many talented dogs in television and movies, there are now dog awards like the Palm Dog Award, the Gold Collar, and the Fidos.

SELENA GOMEZ

Selena Gomez is an actress, singer, and puppy owner! That's right: Selena and Justin Bieber adopted a husky-mix puppy named Baylor from an animal rescue center in Canada. It was true puppy love!

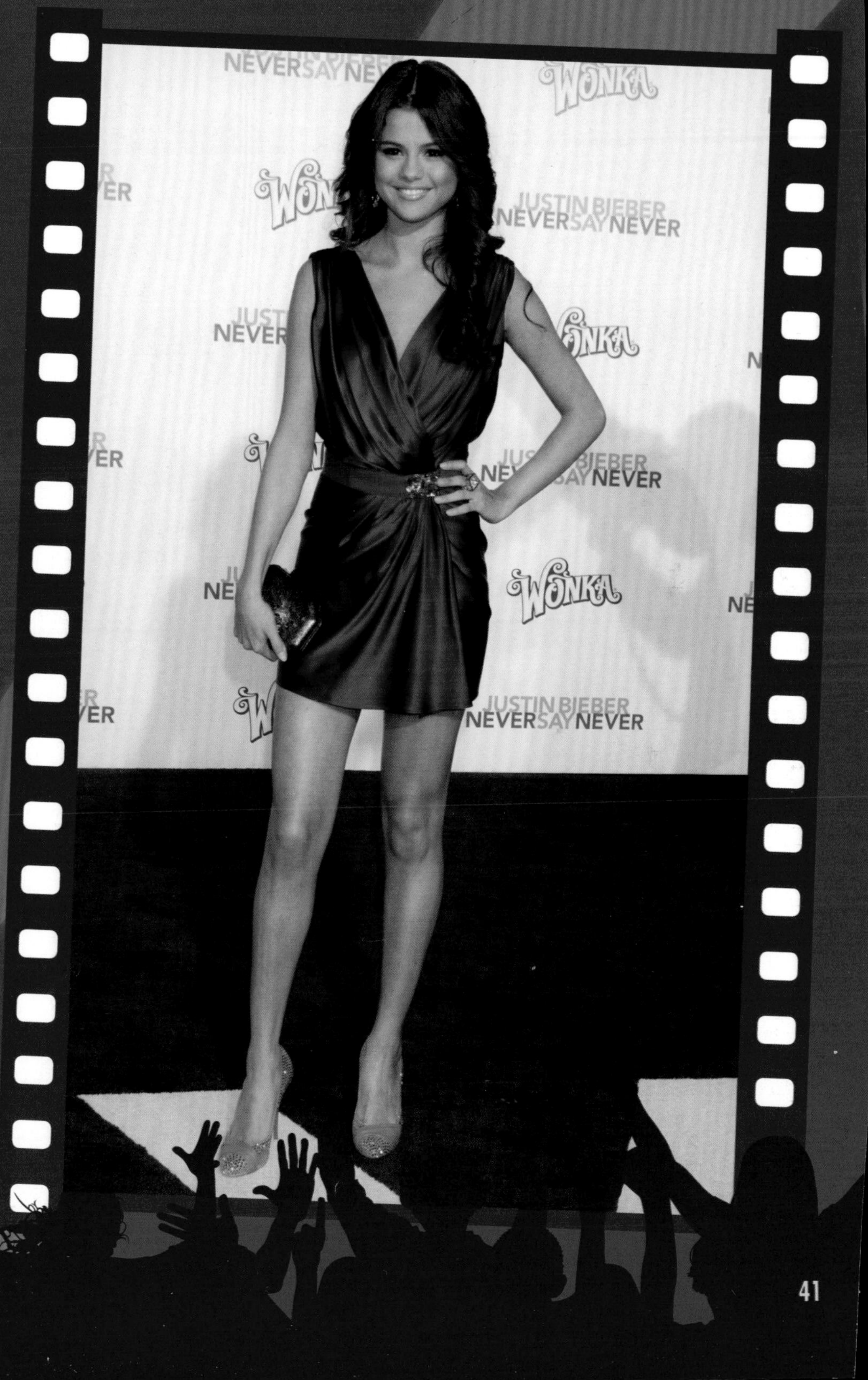
JUSTIN BIEBER
NEVER SAY NEVER
WONKA

BLENHEIM-COLORED CAVALIER KING CHARLES SPANIEL

Some dogs are lucky to have a loving family. Others are in dog shelters waiting for the perfect owner to take them home.

CEE-LO GREEN

Cee-Lo Green is best known for his song "Forget You." As a famous musician and one of the judges on *The Voice*, Cee-Lo has a great ear for music.

BLACK FRENCH BULLDOG

Dogs can hear much better than humans. They also can move their ears closer to the source of a sound thanks to extra muscles in their ears. This lets them hear sounds that are very soft or very far away.

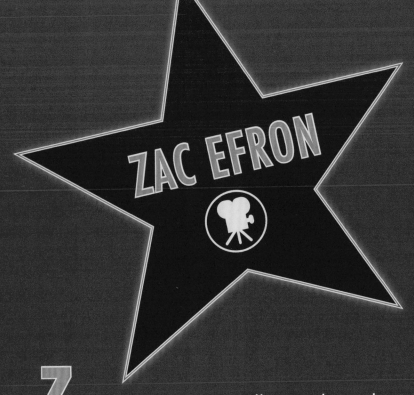

ZAC EFRON

Zac Efron became Hollywood royalty in Disney's *High School Musical* as Troy Bolton. Now Zac is busy acting in even bigger roles and is destined to win awards in the near future. When Zac isn't on set, he loves playing with his loyal pal named Puppy, an Australian shepherd.

The LORAX
TEACHING GARDENS
Dr. Seuss'
The LORAX
Dr. Seuss
The LORAX
TEACHING GARDENS
Dr. Seuss'
The LORAX
TEACHING GARDENS

MI-KI

Every year, dogs compete for Best in Show at the Westminster Kennel Club dog show. Dogs go through hours of grooming to make sure they show off their best features. This competition has been going on since 1877!

KEKE PALMER

At nine years old, Keke Palmer reached celeb status for her performance as the lead role in the movie *Akeelah and the Bee*. Since then she's had her own television show on Nickelodeon and acted in many movies. With such a bright future in front of her, Keke will be on Hollywood's Walk of Fame for sure!

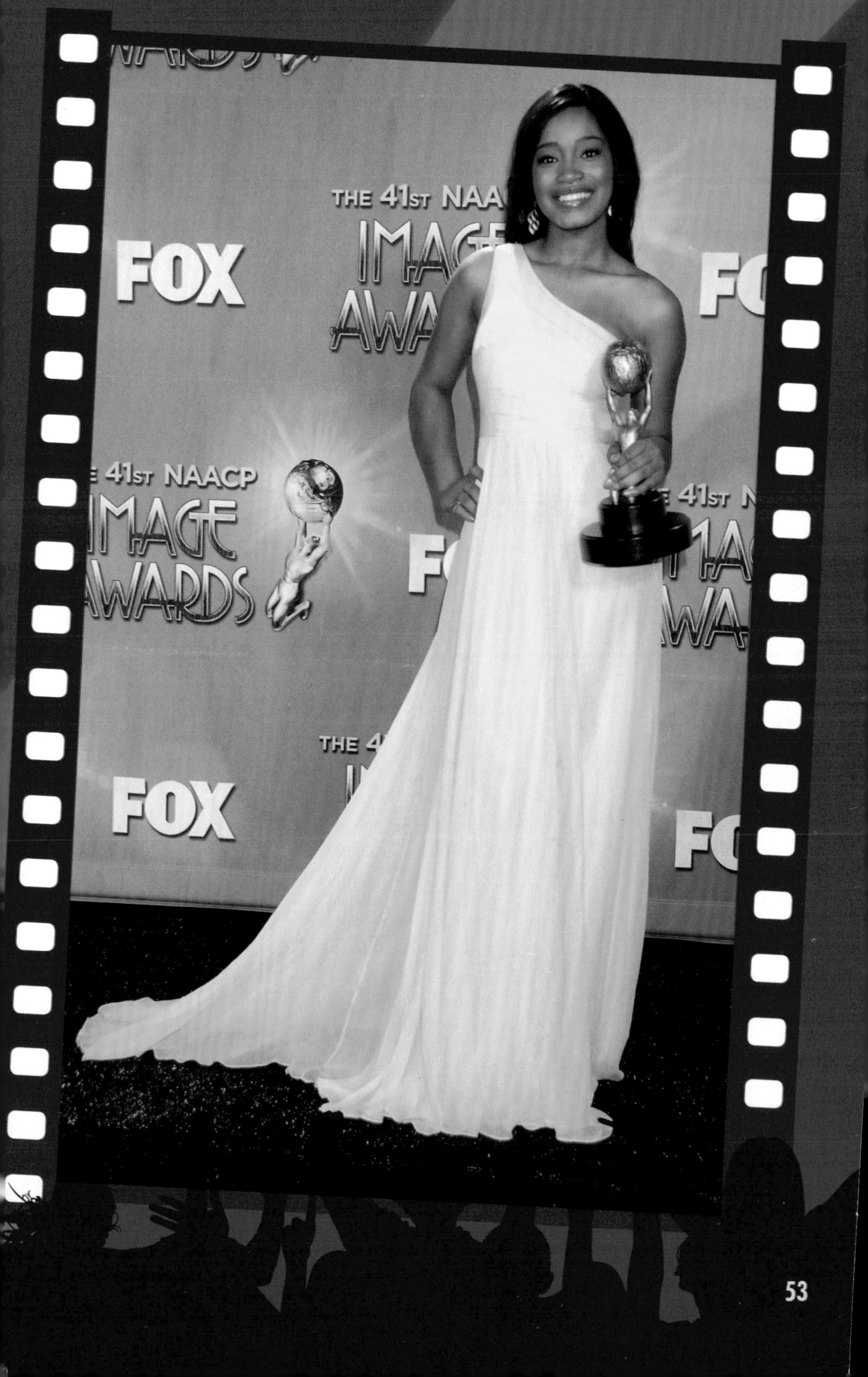
THE 41ST NAACP
IMAGE AWARDS
FOX

MINIATURE DACHSHUND

The Hollywood Walk of Fame isn't just for humans—three dogs have been honored with their own stars on the famous pavement. These three lucky pooches are Lassie, Strongheart, and Rin Tin Tin.

JENNIFER LOPEZ

Jennifer Lopez knows how to glam it up in expensive gowns and jewelry. Who's Jennifer Lopez's favorite dog? Pitbull!

TRICOLOR, LONG-HAIRED CHIHUAHUA

One of the most popular dog accessories is the dog collar. The most expensive one ever made is worth $3.2 million! Look out, girls, diamonds are a dog's best friend!

LADY GAGA

Lady Gaga is considered a true artist with her unique style, ever-changing sound, and incredible music videos. The music video for her first big hit, "Poker Face," featured two Great Danes.

PIT BULL

Dogs have been an important part of art for centuries. From Egyptian hieroglyphics to the famous paintings of Pablo Picasso and Andy Warhol, dogs have been an inspiration to many artists.

Whether they are celebrity pets, actors, or just fashion-savvy, all dogs have the chance to shine in the spotlight.